Wheatfield and Cypress Trees, by Vincent van Gogh. 1889, oil on canvas, 72.1 x 90.9 cm. © Art Resource, NY/National Gallery, London, Great Britain, photo by Erich Lessing.

Mont Sainte-Victoire Seen from Bibemus Quarry, by Paul Cézanne. c.1879, oil on canvas, 65.1 x 80 cm. © The Baltimore Museum of Art: The Cone Collection, formed by Dr. Claribel Cone and Miss Etta Cone of Baltimore, Maryland, BMA1950.196.

The Three Dancers, by Pablo Picasso. 1925, oil on canvas, 215.3 x 142.2 cm. © Art Resource, NY/Tate Gallery, London, UK/©2002 Estate of Pablo Picasso/Artists Rights Society (ARS), New York.

Harmony in Red, by Henri Matisse. 1908, oil on canvas, 69 3/4 x 85 7/8 in. © Art Resource, NY/Hermitage, St. Petersburg, Russia/Scala/© Succession H. Matisse, Paris/Artists Rights Society (ARS), New York.

Many famous artists, including Vincent van Gogh, Paul Cézanne, Pablo Picasso, and Henri Matisse, were influenced by Delacroix in one way or another. They all thought he was the greatest.

The Battle of Taillebourg, by Eugène Delacroix. 1837, oil on canvas, 48.5 x 55.5 cm.
© Bridgeman Art Library International Ltd., London/New York,
Chateau de Versailles, France/Giraudon.

Eugène Delacroix's bursts of pure red, blue, lime-green, and gold seemed very new and modern to people of his time. In the early 1800s, most painters used duller, mixed-together colors. Delacroix's brighter colors added an exciting energy to his paintings. But some people thought his splashes of color and energized brush strokes were too shocking to make a good painting.

Just before Eugène Delacroix came along, calmer, prettier paintings were popular in France. Most paintings, like the one above, were created to decorate palaces and wealthy people's homes.

French people also enjoyed scenes from Greek and Roman history. These paintings of ancient times were carefully drawn, with well-balanced compositions that showed very little action.

The Oath of the Horatii, by Jacques Louis David. 1784, oil on canvas, 330 x 425 cm.
© Bridgeman Art Library International Ltd., London/New York, Louvre, Paris, France/Giraudon.

Arab Horses Fighting in a Stable, by Eugène Delacroix. 1860, oil on canvas, 64.6 x 81 cm. © Art Resource, NY/Louvre, Paris, France/Réunion des Musées Nationaux.

De temps en temps j'aime à voir le vieux Père, Et je me garde bien de lui rompre en Visière.

Mephistopheles Aloft, by Eugène Delacroix. 1828, lithograph, 27 x 23 cm. © Art Resource, NY/Réunion des Musées Nationaux/Musée Eugene Delacroix, Paris, France, photo by H. Lewandowski.

Eugène Delacroix's paintings were often filled with action. He loved to show historical battles or animals fighting one another. Delacroix especially enjoyed painting scenes from exciting stories written by his favorite authors.

The Abduction of Rebecca, by Eugène Delacroix. 1846, oil on canvas, 100.3 x 81.9 cm. © Metropolitan Museum of Art, Catharine Lorillard Wolfe Collection, Wolfe Fund, 1903 (03.30).

William Shakespeare, Lord Byron, Robert Burns, Victor Hugo, and Johann Wolfgang von Goethe inspired many of Eugène Delacroix's works. The painting above is a scene from Sir Walter Scott's famous story *Ivanhoe.*

Eugène Delacroix grew up in a pretty wealthy family. His mother came from a family of successful cabinetmakers, and his father was an ambassador.

Eugène told people that his childhood had not been dull. He said he was nearly burned in his bed, nearly drowned in the Port of Marseilles, poisoned, hanged by the neck with a real rope, and almost choked by a bunch of grapes! When he wasn't almost getting killed, Eugène somehow found time to learn to play the piano, violin, and guitar extremely well.

Eugène Delacroix went to one of the best schools in Paris. He was an excellent student, especially in Latin, Greek, and drawing. Eugène made lots of sketches in his notebooks. Once, he made an etching on the bottom of his mother's saucepan.

Eugène Delacroix was lucky to live in Paris. Paris was the home of one of the greatest art museums in the world, the Louvre.

A friend of Delacroix's said that when he and Eugène were only ten years old, they went to the Louvre one day. The sight of all the incredible paintings by famous artists made Eugène Delacroix declare on the spot that he would be a painter.

When Eugène Delacroix was seventeen years old, he entered an art school run by one of the best teachers of the day, Pierre Guérin. Guérin taught the calm, carefully drawn, classical style of painting. Eugène learned a lot about drawing, art history, and painting in Guérin's studio.

Aeneas Telling Dido of the Disaster at Troy, by Baron Pierre-Narcisse Guérin. 1815.
© Bridgeman Art Library International Ltd., London/New York, Louvre, Paris, France/Lauros-Giraudon

He also found the studio an exciting and fun place to be. Students took turns modeling as storybook characters or important historical figures. Many famous artists dropped by to discuss art with the students.

Eugène Delacroix found the work of one visiting artist to be the most interesting he had ever seen. Théodore Géricault was seven years older than Delacroix and had once studied at Pierre Guérin's school.

Eugène and Théodore ended up becoming great friends. Delacroix got to see his friend plan out and create one of the most amazing paintings of the day, *The Raft of the Medusa*.

The *Medusa* was an actual French ship that had sunk off the coast of Africa. Géricault's painting shows a group of shipwrecked people from the *Medusa* the moment they see a rescue ship far in the distance. Géricault showed people's hope and fear in a way that had never been seen before in European art.

The Raft of the Medusa, by Théodore Géricault. 1819, oil on canvas, 491 x 716 cm.
© Bridgeman Art Library International Ltd., London/New York, Louvre, Paris, France.

Théodore Géricault's painting was very successful. People came from all over to see it. It inspired Eugène Delacroix to do a similar type of painting. But instead of using a real-life event, Eugène decided to paint a scene from one of his favorite stories, *Dante's Inferno.* In *The Barque of Dante,* Delacroix began placing brighter colors in just the right places. *The Barque of Dante* was shown at the important Paris Salon art show in 1822.

The Barque of Dante, by Eugène Delacroix. 1822, oil on canvas, 189 x 241.5 cm.
© Bridgeman Art Library International Ltd., London/New York, Louvre, Paris, France.

Some people thought Delacroix's painting was great, while others didn't like it at all. One thing everyone agreed on, though, was that they couldn't wait to see what Eugène Delacroix would come up with next.

No one was disappointed with Delacroix's entries at the next Paris Salon. In one of his paintings, Eugène showed a tragic event that had just happened on the Greek Island of Chios.

The Massacre at Chios, by Eugène Delacroix. 1822, oil on canvas, 41.7 x 35.4 cm. © Bridgeman Art Library International Ltd., London/New York, Louvre, Paris, France/Giraudon.

While Eugène was working on this painting, he saw the work of an English artist named John Constable. Eugène noticed how Constable had used little dabs of bright color to give his painting a feeling of natural sunlight flickering across his scene.

Eugène then went back and added more touches of color to his own painting. The added color gave *The Massacre at Chios* a special liveliness. Years later, this painting would inspire Claude Monet, Pierre Auguste Renoir, and other Impressionist artists.

Eugène Delacroix studied color more and more. Although some people disliked his splashy colors, many others were beginning to realize that Eugène Delacroix was doing something very special in his art. He was using color to express the moods and feelings of his paintings.

A Moroccan Saddling a Horse, by Eugène Delacroix. 1855, oil on canvas, 56 x 47 cm.
© Bridgeman Art Library International Ltd., London/New York, Hermitage, St. Petersburg, Russia.

The Lion Hunt, Study of Arabs on Horseback, by Eugène Delacroix. 1855-56, oil on canvas, 57 x 74 cm.
© Statens Konstmuseer/National Museum of Fine Arts, Sweden, Hans Thorwid.

One subject Delacroix always enjoyed painting was wild animals. He loved the power and energy he saw in tigers, panthers, jaguars, and lions. Eugène was always going to the zoo in Paris to study animals for his paintings.

A Young Tiger Playing with its Mother, by Eugène Delacroix. 1830, oil on canvas, 130.5 x 195 cm. © Art Resource, NY/Louvre, Paris, France, photo by Erich Lessing.

When he couldn't make it to the zoo, Eugène was quite happy to use his own pet cat as a model for a ferocious lion or tiger.

Group of Cavaliers and a View of Meknes, from "Album of a Voyage to Spain, Morocco and Algeria," by Eugène Delacroix. 1832, watercolor and pencil on paper. © Bridgeman Art Library International Ltd., London/New York, Musée Conde, Chantilly, France.

Head of a Young Girl with a Scarf, Two Girls at their Toilet, at Tangiers, from "Carnet du Maroc" by Eugène Delacroix. 1832, watercolor and pencil on paper. © Bridgeman Art Library International Ltd., London/New York, Musée Conde, Chantilly, France.

In 1832, when Eugène Delacroix was thirty-four years old, he got the chance of a lifetime. Eugène was invited to go on a trip to Morocco. At that time, Morocco was a kingdom in North Africa.

When he got there, Eugène saw beautiful pink and white buildings surrounded by palm trees. The magical sunsets and the ancient costumes of the people made Morocco seem like a mysterious storybook land.

The Women of Algiers in their Apartment, by Eugène Delacroix. 1834, oil on canvas, 180 x 229 cm.
© Bridgeman Art Library International Ltd., London/New York, Louvre, Paris, France/Giraudon.

Eugène made tons of sketches in his notebooks. Although he didn't make any oil paintings on his trip, he used the sketches as ideas for paintings when he returned to Paris.

For many years, Eugène Delacroix put all his efforts into painting huge murals for the ceilings and walls of palaces, libraries, hotels, and churches. In 1850, he was given the honor of painting ceiling murals in his favorite museum, the Louvre! Eugène Delacroix must have been proud to have his work in the same museum as many of the world's greatest masterpieces.

Alexander Preserves Homer's Poems, by Eugène Delacroix. 1846, oil on remounted canvas, 680 cm diameter. © French Senate, Communication Service.

Apollo Vanquishing Python, central panel from the Gallery of Apollo, by Eugène Delacroix. 1850-51,
oil on mounted canvas, 800 x 750 cm. © Art Resource, NY/Réunion des Musées Nationaux, Louvre, Paris, France,
photo by G. Blot/C. Jean.

Eugène Delacroix died in Paris at the age of sixty-five. Delacroix wasn't afraid to experiment with his paintings. He took chances with his action-filled compositions, exciting brushwork, and daring colors. Eugène Delacroix created unforgettable paintings that led the way to the world of modern art.

Works of art in this book can be seen at the following places:

The Art Institute of Chicago
The Baltimore Museum of Art
Hermitage Museum, St. Petersburg
Louvre, Paris
The Metropolitan Museum of Art, New York
Musée Conde, Chantilly
Musée Eugène Delacroix, Paris
National Gallery, London
National Museum of Fine Arts, Stockholm
Saint Louis Art Museum
Tate Gallery, London